Original title:
From Floor to Ceiling

Copyright © 2025 Creative Arts Management OÜ
All rights reserved.

Author: Victor Mercer
ISBN HARDBACK: 978-1-80587-041-8
ISBN PAPERBACK: 978-1-80587-511-6

Stairways of Memory

On the first step, a sock appears,
A lost moment from yesteryear.
The second rung, a forgotten snack,
Topped with crumbs and tiny flak.

Each level climbs with silly sights,
A rubber chicken takes its flights.
At the top, I find my slippers,
Laughing softly as time slivers.

Skylight Serenade

In the bright light, a moth's ballet,
Doing the cha-cha in broad day.
The cat leaps up, with grace and flair,
Only to tumble like a hair.

Sunbeams twirl like a funky dance,
While dust bunnies join in the chance.
A giggle escapes from the corner wall,
As shadows trip, then start to fall.

Echoes of Elevation

The elevator goes up and down,
With every jolt, we wear a frown.
An old tune squeaks from the box,
Just like my socks, they need some locks.

A voice calls out from high above,
Don't get stuck; just wear your glove!
With every stop, a story tall,
The echo of laughter fills the hall.

Climbing through Time

Step by step, we watch the clock,
Each tick is like a funny knock.
We pause on a stair, giggles break,
Remembering when we faked a quake.

The years fly by in a silly race,
As we dodge dust in the open space.
Old memories cling like childish glue,
As we sway, reminiscing what we knew.

The Architecture of Dreams

In a house made of candy, oh what a sight,
Gumdrop windows and frosting, pure delight.
The jellybean stairs lead up to the moon,
And licorice railings make me swoon.

Every room filled with laughter and glee,
Chocolate fountains flow endlessly.
Cupcake chairs that bounce with a smile,
I'd live here forever, just for a while.

Skylines and Grounded Tales

I once had a friend who flew in a shoe,
He thought it was stylish, and so did his crew.
They'd zip through the rooftops, causing a ruckus,
With shoelaces tied, no one could stop us.

At night, they would land on a sandwich parade,
Dancing on pickles, all part of the game.
They'd bonk heads with pigeons, joke about heights,
Then laugh as the stars turned on their lights.

Ascendancy of the Heart

There's a ladder made of spaghetti and cheese,
Climbing it slowly is quite the tease.
But each step up brings a cheerful cheer,
As meatballs roll down, far from here.

I climbed to the clouds on a maple syrup train,
With passengers giggling, going insane.
They told silly stories of things they had seen,
And how they'd once danced with a pickle queen.

Footsteps Beneath Stardust

Beneath the night sky, we danced on thin air,
With socks full of stardust, a whimsical flare.
Our feet tapped to rhythms of cosmic delight,
As stars winked and sparkled, oh what a night!

We tripped on the moonbeams, fell up to the sun,
Each tumble and giggle made life more fun.
Frolicking past planets, we swirled and we spun,
In this silly ballet, we danced everyone.

The Pulse of the Vertical

The cat climbed high, oh what a sight,
With every leap, she took to flight.
A shelf of knick-knacks, all in a mess,
It turns out she loves to play princess.

Books toppled down, a majestic fall,
Her throne of chaos, the finest of all.
The dog looked up, and gave a sigh,
'Here we go again, oh me, oh my!'

Uplifting Perspectives

The ceiling fans spin, round and round,
Chasing the dust like it was profound.
A bird flew in; it seemed quite lost,
In a dance with the shadows, no matter the cost.

The plants all gathered for a concert today,
Singing their leaves in a breezy ballet.
The light bulbs flickered, lost in the beat,
As laughter erupted from an old wooden seat.

Beyond the Limits

The ladder stood tall, a challenge to climb,
With rickety steps, it's no mountain to mime.
A squirrel perched up, holding an acorn,
Mocking my efforts, oh how I felt worn!

The ceiling beams whispered secrets of grace,
While I awkwardly fumbled, losing my place.
Who knew home could host such a show?
With every misstep, it answered, 'Just go with the flow!'

The Untold Altitude

The balloon floated, a bright little sphere,
Making a bid for the atmosphere near.
With giggles and grins, kids chased it around,
While it danced on air, joyfully unbound.

A kite flew past, waving 'hello,'
As I tripped on the rug, putting on a show.
The room burst with laughter, a circus of fun,
It's hard to stay down when the ceiling's the sun!

Echoes of Heights and Depths

In the attic, dust bunnies dance,
While the chair creaks in a trance.
A mouse with a hat sings the blues,
Chasing dreams in mismatched shoes.

The basement's home to forgotten socks,
Vengeful shadows and rusty locks.
A laundry basket, a knight so brave,
Defending realms from a tumble's wave.

Vertical Whispers

Up on the shelf, a cat plots schemes,
Holding court with the kings of dreams.
The fish in the bowl shakes its head,
While the slippers plot what to wear to bed.

The ceiling fan spins tales of the past,
Sneaking secrets and laughter vast.
With each twirl, a giggle slips through,
As the light bulbs wink in playful cue.

Ascent of Shadows

The stairs are alive with the squeak of shoes,
As shadows compete in an awkward cruise.
A toddler tumbles, making it keen,
In a race with the cat who's oh-so-mean.

The wall clocks chuckle, they tickle time,
While the dust on the ledge claims a life of grime.
All while the broom gives a gentle shove,
Whispering sweetly, "Let's dance, my love!"

The Space Between Stripes

In the laundry, chaos reigns supreme,
Colors clash, in an unearthly dream.
The white shirts whisper, 'We're not so plain,'
While the reds shout, 'Join our revolution reign!'

Towels drape like capes of laughter,
The dryer hums, 'I'm your happy ever after.'
In the space between garments, they plot and scheme,
Hatching plans to burst the seams of the dream!

Vertical Dreams Unraveled

In a world where slippers reign,
I failed to notice the windowpane.
My plants have grown, oh what a sight,
They're reaching high for all their might.

A cat named Whiskers thinks he's king,
He rules the shelves, of that, I sing.
He jumps and tumbles, oh so grand,
While I just watch, my coffee in hand.

Ascending Aspirations

I climbed the ladder, step by step,
To reach the cookies on the prep.
But gravity's a pesky friend,
And down I went, with cookie blend.

My ceiling fan spins tales of woe,
As I try to dodge the dust below.
I'm in the air, a dizzy bird,
With only one thing, just one, absurd.

The View from Below

Peeking under the couch, a sight!
Old socks and crumbs, oh what a fright.
The dust bunnies leap with joy and glee,
At the tale of my lost laundry spree.

I spot a shoe, from days long past,
Another one vanished, found at last.
I wave it high, a victory small,
With every find, I stand tall.

Between the Layers

In the depths of my closet, a war does brew,
With clothes that no longer fit, quite askew.
A bright pink sweater, oh so loud,
Challenging me to wear it proud.

At the back, a treasure trove,
My high school jeans, forever unchove.
Their time has passed, but what the heck,
I'll try them on, and risk the wreck.

Stories Along the Wall

There's a picture of a cat,
Wearing a tiny hat,
It leans and snoozes bright,
While dreams take flight.

A shelf holds shoes so strange,
All with color and range,
One pair sings a tune,
Under the silver moon.

Sticky notes with jokes abound,
On which everyone's spellbound,
They giggle and they cheer,
So glad they're all here!

The wall clock ticks away cheer,
With faces that sure leer,
It knows all the time,
When silly is in prime.

In The Shadow of the Beams

Underneath the beams so high,
Ants march in a parade, oh my!
One dons a little cape,
In a bug-sized escape.

The ceiling fan spins and grins,
Whisking away dust and sins,
It hums a tune out loud,
Making the light dance proud.

Between the snacks and stacked books,
Frogs in pajamas give funny looks,
They hop on the table, you see,
Making quite the ruckus, whee!

In this house of beams and shade,
Joy's made with every trade,
With laughter that resides,
In giggles that confides.

Foundations of Whimsy

On wobbly chairs with paint so bright,
We laugh and giggle through the night,
Foundations built of jokes and games,
With warmth and peace as flame.

Beneath the stairs, a raccoon hides,
In socks of stripes, it boldly glides,
With a treasure pile of old gum,
Its best friend? A rubber drum.

Walls adorned with sticky art,
Every colorful, quirky part,
Kids' splatters echo memories,
Bursting forth like wild, sweet trees.

So we stack our dreams to reach,
The ceiling's whispers, they can teach,
To laugh aloud, be smart and silly,
Life's a party, really, really!

Viewing Life's Layers

Layers of laughter fill the air,
Like socks mismatched without a care,
We peel them back with each new joke,
As tickles burst and laughter spoke.

Beneath the couch, there hides a shoe,
With stories that it once knew,
How it danced in puddles deep,
Now lone and lost, not a peep.

The window's glare plays hide and seek,
And gives the curtain a little tweak,
It dances with the breezy flow,
Playing games of ebb and glow.

So up we climb, to higher sights,
With giggles echoing through nights,
Each layer found, a joy to share,
In our funny, wild affair!

Ceilings of Hope

In a room filled with dreams, we all aim high,
We bounce on our beds, hoping to touch the sky.
But the ceiling laughs back, all sturdy and tall,
While we're just here leaping, like kites in a brawl.

With tape and some string, we form a grand plan,
To build a tall tower, just think like a Stan.
But woodpeckers giggle, and they peck our contraptions,
As our dreams go a-flutter, their beat steals our actions.

Grounded Reflections

Looking down from my chair, what sights do I find?
A penguin-shaped rug, becoming quite blind.
It giggles and wiggles just like my old pup,
As I sit here and ponder, should I give it a sup?

The floor's an odd canvas, where crumbs lie in wait,
Each one tells a story, like breadcrumbs on fate.
With the dust bunnies dancing, a whimsical crew,
They launch into the air—oh, what mischief they do!

Rise and Embrace

I stretch for the light, with my arms like a star,
But in the tight corner, I've come a bit far.
I trip on my socks, and I tumble with ease,
Like a clumsy old octopus trying to tease.

Imagine the ceiling, a friend made of glue,
Sticking dreams to the tops—what a zany zoo!
With the laughter of echoes, they bounce off the walls,
Inviting my folly, when adventure calls.

The Journey Skyward

Climbing up on the chair, I go for a climb,
To reach for the stars, what a whimsical crime!
The cat gives a meow, saying this isn't wise,
But I just want heights where the laughter can rise.

The chandelier swings, like it's dancing in glee,
As I balance on tiptoes, a sight that must be.
Needing wings like a bird, I prepare for a flight,
Only to discover, I'd rather sit tight!

Reaching for the Stars

A cat on the shelf, oh what a sight,
It leans and it wobbles, not grasping quite right.
The lamp casts a glow, giving light to the fall,
As the cat swats a moth, oh, a comical sprawl.

Dancing on tables, a monkey in dreams,
He swings and he twirls, or so it seems.
Reaching for snacks, with bananas in tow,
The comedy rises as laughter will flow.

Depths and Heights Intertwined

A ladder's beneath, with a squeak and a shudder,
While up on the top, there's a soft peanut butter.
The ceiling fan spins, as if caught in a race,
And jars full of jelly? A sticky embrace!

A fish in a bowl, the ceiling's its star,
It dreams of the sky, oh how bizarre!
With a jump and a flap, it thinks it can fly,
While I vacuum below, thinking, 'Why oh why?'

Memories Against the Plaster

Picture frames hung, a crooked parade,
Each memory whispers, 'We're never delayed!'
A typo in paint, a story we tell,
The laughter erupts as it sticks like a spell.

Old friends in the corners, with giggles anew,
They peek past the wallpaper, with laughter as glue.
Nostalgia is plastered, a messy old trace,
As we trip on the past, but we shimmer with grace.

A Symphony of Surfaces

The floor here is squeaky, a melody bright,
While walls sing of stories from morning till night.
A rug with a dance, the table's a tune,
And the kitchen hums softly beneath the big moon.

Each creak brings a chuckle, each laugh a refrain,
As the fridge hums a ballad, of pickles in vain.
With laughter as rhythm, the ceiling does sway,
In a home full of joy, it's a merrily played.

The Song of Heights and Depths

In a room where clocks are late,
And chairs dance when I'm not straight,
The cat sings to the cozy couch,
While socks plot against the grouchy ouch.

Lamps flicker like they know a joke,
The coffee pot is quite the spoke,
Of tales about the fridge's snore,
And how it hides my snacks galore!

Walls are leaning, playing tricks,
As I stumble on my shoe's quick fix,
The ceiling laughs, it knows my plight,
In this topsy-turvy, silly night.

So here's to height and depth's embrace,
Where all things wobble, dance, and race,
With every step, we lift and fall,
In the grandest jest of all!

Spaces Between the Moments

In the gaps where laughter hides,
And hiccups burst like ocean tides,
I trip on air and hit a wall,
While jumping for a snack, I sprawl.

Between the tick and tasteless tock,
I find a dance among the clock,
The dust bunnies wiggle with glee,
As they mock my lack of grace, oh me!

Glimpses of joy in every breath,
Turn mundane paths to comedic depth,
For just when I start to rest,
A cereal box puts me to the test.

These spaces flutter like a jest,
With life's absurd absurdity dressed,
In moments where I lose my hold,
The funniest stories are retold!

Pathways to the Ethereal

Through hallways where the echoes play,
And slippers take off on their own way,
I chase a shadow with a grin,
That leaps and bounds, let the fun begin!

Stairs that giggle when I trip,
And landing pads, they never skip,
As each step leads to a new surprise,
While ceiling beams are watching wise.

In corners where my jokes are planned,
And every picture has a hand,
That mocks my silly, silly moves,
While the broom dances to improve!

A journey where the laughter flows,
Underneath the light that glows,
So let's embark on this delight,
And never stop, not even at night!

Navigating the Vertical Vortex

In a spiral where the cats take flight,
And hats have meanings that excite,
I balance on the edge of fun,
As climbing walls weigh a ton!

The ceiling spins in a dizzy dance,
While I attempt a silly prance,
The floor jumps up to touch the sky,
As pillows form a fortress, oh my!

Navigating this chaotic mess,
Where toys and laughter coalesce,
Each tumble tells a funny tale,
Of mischief wrapped in a cardboard sail.

So join this ride, let's take a peek,
At all the quirks that make us weak,
In this spiral of giggles and grace,
Life's vertical vortex is our place!

In the Embrace of Enclosed Spaces

In tiny rooms, we dance and twirl,
Our laughter echoes, a joyful swirl.
Legs twist and turn, bumping the walls,
We'll never fit in those little stalls.

The fridge is a throne in this grand domain,
Where yogurt jokes make us go insane.
A couch so small, we cuddle and squeeze,
In this close-knit space, we find our ease.

The door creaks open, what a surprise,
A game of dodgeball, oh how time flies.
Under the table, a treasure we find,
Lost socks and snacks, all intertwined.

Our space is cozy, but oh so tight,
We battle for space in the flickering light.
Yet in this chaos, hugs and delight,
We find sweet solace in our shared plight.

Treading the Ascending Spiral

Up we go on this wobbly stair,
Each step a giggle, as we declare.
"Not so fast!" as we trip and roll,
The spiral's a charmer that takes its toll.

In rubbery shoes, we glide and sway,
Who knew a staircase could lead to play?
Caught in a whirlwind of dizzy shows,
We leap and laugh, like giddy pros.

With every twist, a new chance to fall,
We bob like balloons against the wall.
A staircase to nowhere, but oh what fun,
Chasing gravity, we sprint and run.

Let's take a selfie on this wild ride,
Our smiles are wide, our arms open wide.
Up to the top, then back down we fly,
On this merry path, we can't say goodbye!

Strokes of Elevation

With paintbrush ready, we color the air,
Splashes of humor, no need to beware.
Up on the ladder, a splash too bold,
My masterpiece? A chaos uncontrolled.

The ceiling's a canvas, we're making it stick,
But here comes the puddle! Oh, what a trick!
Drips and drops turn to giggles galore,
We're artists of mayhem, want even more.

One stroke of blue, followed by red,
Oops! there goes my helper, off with a spread.
The floor now a rainbow, a slippery sight,
Creativity blossoms, oh what a delight!

Our strokes of madness, they rise and they fall,
Each color a story, echoing our call.
In the chaos of art, we laugh and play,
Transforming our space in a whimsical way.

Reaching Beyond the Limitations

Jumping and bouncing, we're breaking the mold,
On furniture peaks, we brave and bold.
The sofa a mountain, we claim the throne,
In this kingdom of cushions, we're not alone.

Pretending to fly, we swing from the lamps,
Navigating this jungle, avoiding the clamps.
Watch out for the cat, she guards the hall,
With her watchful eye, she plans our downfall.

We stretch and we bend, defying the norm,
Inventing wild games that break from the form.
In each little nook, laughter takes flight,
With no limits in sight, we dance through the night.

So here's to the dreams in our cramped little space,
Where antics abound and we quicken our pace.
With every attempt, we conquer the day,
In the laughter and chaos, we'll always stay.

A Tapestry of Heights

In a house of unexpected drapes,
Cats are plotting their escapes.
Each curtain rod a climbing spree,
As they dance like acrobats, oh me!

I tripped over the vacuum today,
It looked like it wanted to play.
Spinning like a topsy-tailed toy,
I yelled 'To infinity!' like a boy.

The chandelier swings with a laugh,
A shiny orb from the ceiling staff.
Hanging jests from each silver thread,
With luminous giggles that wake the dead.

Mice in hats throw a rave down low,
While shadows on the walls put on a show.
As if the house tried to flip on its head,
In this crazy world where everyone's fed.

Celestial Boundaries

The ceiling's calling, I swear it sings,
Glittering with an angel's wings.
While I reach for snacks on the top shelf's edge,
Cereal tumbles, teetering like a hedge.

My dog thinks he's a space-bound prince,
Jumping high and doing a spin.
Each leap a quest for the Milky Way,
While the couch laughs, it can't get away.

The wallpaper wiggles, a colorful tease,
Patterns that shift in the playful breeze.
I swear it winks when I'm not around,
In rooms where silliness knows no bound.

Brooms parade like a witch's crew,
As I dodge the signs of things overdue.
A dance party erupts with a broomstick twist,
In my home, cosmic fun can't be missed.

Archways of Imagination

An archway whispers tales of delight,
Where shadows pirouette in the night.
Mice wield flashlights made from cheese,
In this place, laughter rides the breeze.

Each doorway leads to a world of dreams,
Where nothing is truly as it seems.
A trampoline hides beneath the rug,
Bouncing my worries with a little hug.

The hall's a slide, who needs a park?
With every step, a playful spark.
On cupboards filled with surprises galore,
Each opening a chance to explore.

With chairs transformed into rocket ships,
We zoom to space with silly quips.
And when we land, it's time for pie,
In a home where imagination can fly.

In the Grip of Gravity

With gravity pulling down on my head,
I often find my socks misled.
They tango together, slipping on floors,
While I navigate impossible chore wars.

The ceiling fan spins like a cheerful friend,
As I ponder where this mess might end.
A leaf floats down like it's taking a dip,
In the air, I'm planning my next trip.

Plates in the cupboard silently scheme,
To join forces in a balancing dream.
I reach for a glass, it cuts loose and shatters,
While gravity chuckles, 'It doesn't matter!'

In this house of mayhem and cheer,
Every plummet's a laugh, never fear.
With every tumble and every trip,
Life dances wildly, a zany trip!

Echoes in the Eaves

Up in the rafters, a squirrel's delight,
He's hoarding the nuts, in the dead of night.
Poking around, with a curious flair,
Wondering who left those crumbs up in air.

The dust bunnies twirl, a ballet so grand,
They dance with the shadows, hand in hand.
A sock's gone rogue, escaping the pair,
While old shoes yell, 'Hey, you forgot us! Care?'

Mice share tales of the crumbs left behind,
In a world where laughter's the best kind of find.
With echoes of giggles above our heads,
Household dramas unfold where everyone treads.

So raise a toast to the chaos and cheer,
For the madness above brings fun down here!
Skimming through memories, some lost, some found,
Echoes make music where silliness abounds.

Interiors of the Soul

In the hallway, shoes create quite a scene,
A flip-flop chorus, a loafer routine.
While jackets debate, on hangers they hang,
'What's the best style? Let's re-arrange!'

Mirrors whisper secrets, tales of the past,
Reflecting the moments that fly by so fast.
A mop gripes aloud, 'I'm tired and wet!'
While the broom stands proud, 'I'm not done yet!'

The kitchen's alive, pots fight for the shelf,
Spatulas giggle, 'Let's stir up some help!'
Fridges hum low, with a contented sigh,
While leftovers giggle and quietly lie.

So here's to the joy in the clamor and clank,
To the jests of the inanimate, giving a prank.
For in this space, where chaos does dwell,
Lies laughter and warmth, and stories to tell.

Ethereal Journeys

A ceiling fan spins, like a ship on the seas,
Surging through rooms with a playful tease.
Curtains flutter, a ghostly ballet,
Whispers of draughts come to dance and play.

Light bulbs flicker, they flirt and they feed,
On the brightness of laughter, igniting a need.
A clock ticks its jokes, 'Time's but a game!'
While socks on the floor yell, 'We're not the same!'

Paint peels with pride, telling stories of old,
While wallpapers chuckle, their patterns so bold.
A chair creaks with wisdom, 'Sit down if you may,'
As floors tell remembrances of feet at play.

In these ethereal journeys, laughter takes flight,
With each twist and turn, bringing joy to the night.
A toast to the mischief, the highs and the lows,
Where every good moment in space truly grows.

Unfolding the Vertical

A ladder leans back, tired of its task,
It dreams of the heights, it's gone there to bask.
The roof's like a hat, placed slightly askew,
While chimneys hum tunes, old-fashioned but new.

Step by step up, where the wild things play,
A cat spies a bird, plotting mischief today.
And the attic's a world where the oddities bloom,
Like a forgotten sweater, now dressed as a broom.

Walls hold the laughter, and doodles so bright,
Portraying the moments, from day into night.
A gleeful alliance of stories unfolds,
As flapping curtains share secrets untold.

So here's to the upward, the laughter, the clang,
In spaces where echoes of joy still rang.
For in every nook, where the fun findings cling,
Unfolds a tall tale that makes the heart sing.

Heights of Solitude

In the attic I found a hat,
Worn by a cat, imagine that!
Tangled in cobwebs, I danced a jig,
With a broom as my partner, feeling big.

Walls whispered secrets, old and wise,
While I tried to find a pair of ties.
The window stared at the neighbor's cat,
As I pondered where I tossed my spat.

On a shelf, a sock peeked out,
Wondering why I had no doubt.
I laughed with dust bunnies, oh what joy,
In this space, I'm both girl and boy.

Chasing shadows, my imagination flew,
Each creak in the beams told me what's true.
Solitude's height played just like me,
Life's a stage in this comedy.

The Canvas of the Inner World

In a closet, I found my grand design,
Half-finished paintings, none quite divine.
Socks taking selfies, shoes in a stare,
I laughed at the chaos that filled the air.

An old mirror told me tales, it's clear,
Of hairdos gone wild and far too sheer.
I painted the walls with colors so bright,
My imagination soared, a comical sight.

Books piled high like a wobbly tower,
As I reached for one, it rained like flour.
A mighty mess, a flurry of fun,
In this playful mess, I am never done.

The canvas inside not a chore to mold,
Each stroke a giggle, a story retold.
The art of my thoughts, a circus so grand,
In the playful chaos, I make my stand.

Touching What Lies Above

With a stick, I reached for a lingering shoe,
It danced like a bird, who knew it could do?!
Higher I climbed, with a grin on my face,
To touch the horizon, a thrilling chase.

I swung from the light, a champion of fun,
Pretending to fly, oh, look at me run!
The ceiling had secrets I longed to embrace,
As I zigzagged around in this limitless space.

A bird in a cage, just a sock on the wall,
They laughed at my antics, I'd hope for a call.
"Hey buddy, come chat!" —a whisper it seemed,
But all that I heard was a chew and a dreamed.

So up I went, with nothing to fear,
To dance with the shadows that tickled my ear.
What lies above was a treasure of jest,
Each "oops!" and "oh no!" made me feel blessed.

The Silent Witness

A chair in the corner just giggled with glee,
As I tripped on the rug and yelled, "Look at me!"
It witnessed the laughter of moments gone by,
As I sprawled on the floor, wishing to fly.

The clock on the wall ticked a funny beat,
Its hands waved hello, not missing a greet.
"Oh, time, take a break!" I cried with delight,
While cushions erupted in pillows of light.

Peeking through curtains, the sunlight did play,
Chasing away shadows that tried to stay.
The walls chuckled softly, a whisper so sweet,
In this room full of memories, life felt complete.

So here in this space, with its silent refrain,
Laughter echoed louder than any old pain.
Each witness a keeper of joy and of fun,
In this quiet domain, we all came undone.

The Architecture of Remembering

In the attic, old hats stack,
Worn by folks who never look back.
A collection of giggles, a dance on the wall,
Each memory echoes, each story a call.

Creaky stairs carry whispers of fun,
Laughter erupts like a well-timed pun.
Dust bunnies gather with secrets to share,
They've seen all the dance moves, if only they dare.

Pictures hang crooked, like faces in jest,
Mismatched frames harbor dreams of the best.
Walls hold the laughter, the ups and the downs,
Each corner a kingdom, of kings and of clowns.

So let's raise our glasses to rooms full of cheer,
To the moments that stick, to the joy we hold dear.
In the architecture of life, let's take a sweet peek,
At the funny old stories that play hide-and-seek.

Shadows at Dusk

Shadows stretch long as the sun takes a bow,
A flip-flop dance on the sill, oh wow!
Creeping around, they trip up my thoughts,
Making me giggle at all the strange knots.

There's a chair that has seen a fair bit of pain,
Cushioned so soft, yet it proudly looks plain.
Sitting with snacks, it just can't complain,
A throne for the zany king of the grain.

Socks without partners just hop on the floor,
Looking for dance partners forevermore.
The curtain gives way to a waltz and a spin,
While shadows play tag, and laughter creeps in.

At dusk all the silliness starts to take flight,
With flickering lights and a dash of pure light.
Let's gather the giggles before they disperse,
In the realm of the funny, we're all in reverse.

Beyond the Vertical

Up on the ladder, I reach for the stars,
With paint on my nose and my friends in charge.
They're trying to help, but end up in a blur,
As we splash on colors that cause quite a stir.

A ceiling fan spins, looking dizzy and dazed,
Cheering us on, but feeling quite phased.
It whispers sweet nothings, like a sass in the air,
"Who knew painting walls could lead to this flair?"

The floors keep on squeaking with laughter and glee,
Every step a mishap, oh will there ever be,
A moment of silence, or calmness, or peace?
Instead, just the echo of friendships that increase.

We laugh and we paint, we dance and we sing,
Creating a world that only we bring.
Beyond all that's vertical, let laughter be free,
In this topsy-turvy home of hilarity!

Bridging Burdens

A bridge made of pillows connects the lost socks,
With hugs from the cushions and soft-spoken clocks.
Each step is a bounce, with giggles galore,
While creatures of fluff plan mischief in store.

On one side, the laundry piles high with a grin,
On the other, remote controls tossed in a spin.
What lives on this bridge? A parade of old socks,
Who march to the rhythm of wash cycle clocks.

Weights of the world are just feathers to share,
When humor entwines every burden and care.
Together we carry each giggle so bright,
Turning woes into joy, making everything light.

So let's build our bridge, let the laughter run wild,
With whimsy and wonder, let us all be a child.
In the dance of our burdens, we find our release,
With chuckles and joy, we discover our peace.

Carved Milestones

Each step a story, carved and quaint,
With laughter echoing, oh, so feint.
A sock on a stair, it flies like a kite,
 Chasing the dog into the night.

The cat on a ledge, looking quite grand,
Judging my balance with a flick of her hand.
I stumble and laugh, it's all in good fun,
 In this house, the rooftop's just begun.

Lemonade spills at the edge of the floor,
A slippery journey, who could ask for more?
Handprints on walls, I treasure them so,
 Every little mark, a tale on the go.

So dance with the dust, let your spirit soar,
In the heights of the chaos, I find there's more.
Each milestone a chuckle, a peek into glee,
 What a tall tale this life has to be!

Layers of Light

In layers of laughter, we stack up the day,
A rainbow of moments that dance and sway.
Sunbeams peek in, with a curious grin,
Turning the hallway to a jolly din.

Shadows leap forth with a mischievous bite,
Chasing my socks when I turn off the light.
A tickle of giggles from room to room,
As the toaster plugs in, it starts to zoom.

With cookies on shelves that tiptoe and roll,
And a carpet that whispers of old rock and soul.
Light-hearted echoes ascend to the skies,
Splashing bright colors where humor lies.

So let our home sparkle with whimsy and cheer,
For every layer holds stories we hold dear.
In the layers of light, we find our delight,
Flipping the mundane to moments so bright!

Boundless Escalations

Up the great ladder, the fun never stops,
We leap like kangaroos and dodge all the flops.
In a race with the fridge, oh what a sight,
Competing with cats under stars so bright.

The curtains tug down, as if to descend,
Chasing my laughter, my ultimate friend.
Stairs filled with giggles, a climb of pure glee,
Where every corner holds joy that we see.

Bananas slip past with a wink and a smile,
And the vacuum hums its own crazy style.
Reaching up high, we waltz with the air,
In a house built for joy, there's magic to share.

So let's leap with abandon, the ceiling in view,
In the boundless escalations, we'll find something new.
Each step leads us higher, where chuckles abound,
In this whimsical world, true happiness found!

Patterns of the Upward Path

Patterns arise as we stumble and twirl,
A crazy collection, this life's vibrant whirl.
Jellybeans scatter from cupboards above,
While shoes do a jig, it's a dance of pure love.

A mismatched sock, the hall's best-dressed star,
Whispers of mischief, oh, how bizarre!
Each rise in our journey, a bounce and a roll,
In the upward path, every giggle takes toll.

From crumbs on the floor to balloons in flight,
Every little moment just feels so right.
With pillows that bounce and giggly gasps,
In unpredictable places, our joy tightly clasps.

So join in the dance, unleash all your cheer,
For laughter's the ladder that draws us all near.
In patterns of humor, let's lift every heart,
On this joyful journey, we'll never depart!

Looking Upward

I found a moth upon the wall,
It danced like it had won a ball.
With wings so grand, it leapt and twirled,
A tiny star in a giant world.

While pondering what it saw down low,
It wished it could sing along with the glow.
Who knew the ceiling held such delight?
A dance-off party in the dead of night!

Every cobweb spun a story untold,
Of dust bunnies wishing they could be bold.
As I laughed and peered up high,
A rubber chicken began to fly!

With each tumble, the ceiling's charm grew,
Of silly moments and shadows too.
So here's to the fun and the quirks we find,
In the upward gaze of the open mind.

Transcending the Ordinary

A squirrel climbed fast to reach the beam,
While the cat below plotted a cream dream.
In the race for the last slice of toast,
The critters declared a vertical boast!

A hat was tossed to the ceiling fan,
Where it spun like a disco plan.
Balloons floated high, without a care,
While I, on the floor, could only stare.

The clock chimed loud, with a tick and a tock,
As my socks did a jig on the kitchen block.
I'd like to know, what goes on that way?
Is it a carnival up there, night and day?

Eventually, I saw a trend emerge,
A parade of puzzled cats began to surge.
With laughter echoing from high to low,
It seemed the ceiling was the real show!

Metaphors in Motion

An elephant's trunk found the ceiling fan,
Whirring around in a playful plan.
It trumpeted loud, with a giggle or two,
As it spun through the room, oh, what a view!

A ladder became a bridge to the sky,
Where I met an octopus named Pie.
We discussed the weather and who liked to swim,
As our laughter crested, the lights grew dim.

Juggling dreams and a laundry line,
Waking to find socks that weren't even mine.
An upward glance brings a tear of joy,
'Cause even the mundane can be a ploy.

With each quirk caught above my sight,
Ceilings transformed into pure delight.
And life, a circus, spins ever still,
As we chase the giggles, with plenty of will.

The Pulse of the Vertical

When the popcorn popped up high above,
It bounced off the ceiling, like laughter from love.
Falling down like little stars in flight,
Who knew snacks could cause such delight?

Up on a shelf, a rubber duck dreamed,
Of carnival rides and a sky that beamed.
It squawked and waddled, a hilarious scene,
Showering giggles like rain from a bean.

The ceiling lights twinkled in comic glee,
As brooms had a party, oh what a spree!
With mops dressed as princes, a sweeping ballet,
They twirled and chuckled through the entire day.

In this upside-down world, so much to adore,
Every glance up reveals a new score.
So let's keep looking, for laughter we seek,
In the vertical waltz, where the ceiling's chic!

The Embrace of Atmosphere

In the room where the laughter flows,
A dancing chair strikes a pose.
The wall clock giggles, time on the run,
While the ceiling fan hums, 'Let's have some fun!'

A pillow takes flight, soaring so high,
Tickling the curtains, as they flutter by.
The rug plays tag with the feet that tread,
Underneath, a sock puppet dreams of bread.

A shoelace loops, and the table sings,
While coffee cups chatter of all kinds of things.
Draped in cozy chaos, joy fills the air,
In this silly shelter, forget every care!

Every nook has a quirk, every cranny a giggle,
With mischief afoot, you'll start to wiggle.
So pull up a chair and join in the spree,
This space isn't plain; it's pure comedy!

Whispers in the Corners

Beneath the window, a whispering dust,
Collecting secrets, in laughter we trust.
The shadows are pranking, flickering bright,
As they dance with the echoes of giggling light.

Each corner is full of peculiar tales,
Where cobwebs giggle and goodwill prevails.
Old socks in a pile throw a party at night,
While the broom lays down beats—what a sight!

Under the table, a gnome waves hello,
He's been here forever, he's in on the show.
With a wink and a nod, he joins the fun,
As the ticklish chairs can't help but run.

So tiptoe through laughter, and sing with delight,
For the corners hold whispers of joy in the night.
In this delightfully quirky abode,
Every nook is a treasure, a funny story owed!

Skyscrapes of Emotion

The ceiling paints skies in colors so bold,
As my heart does a dance that never gets old.
Lamp shades shake their fringe in merriment loud,
While walls crinkle smiles, all wrapped in a cloud.

A couch told a joke, and the pillows agreed,
In this high-rise of humor, there's plenty to feed.
Table legs prance, keeping rhythm so fine,
As laughter rises up like a glorious vine.

The fridge hums a tune of forgotten delight,
While socks in the drawer plan their next flight.
Even the rug spins in curvy delight,
Waving its fibers, a colorful sight.

In the skyscrapers of feelings, we leap and we swirl,
With joy as our guide, let our imaginations twirl.
For every room holds a story or two,
In this world of encounters, where fun is the glue!

Ladders to Lost Realities

Up the rungs, I reach for dreams,
But they slip like yogurt, it seems.
One foot missed, I tumble down,
Chasing thoughts like a clown's frown.

My ladder's shaky, sways in air,
I'm climbing high; a daring dare!
But reaching clouds, I hit my head,
On reality's concrete bed.

Each step I take asks for a fee,
A humor tax? Just let me be!
So on I go, a wobbly spree,
The universe laughs, and so do we.

In this ascent of whimsy's quest,
I find the fun is truly best.
With every fall, a chuckle sprouts,
Who knew life's ladders had such clouts?

Through the Spectrum of Space

I float through hues, a laugh so bright,
In cosmic pants, I take to flight.
A purple smile, a yellow pout,
In space's game, it's all about.

I trip on stardust, what a sight,
With alien socks, oh what a night!
They say to bend the rules to play,
As moons wink back in a cheeky sway.

Planets dance like they just don't care,
While I'm over here, with hair everywhere.
Gravity's lost, it's taken a break,
As I do a twirl by a comet's wake.

In the spectrum wild, we laugh and scream,
For cosmic jest is a lasting theme.
We float through space, in colors bold,
This quirky journey never gets old.

Tethered to Earth

I'm grounded here, but dreams take flight,
With sock puppets singing all night.
My feet are stuck, yet still I soar,
With spaghetti arms, I search for more.

A dancing snail in a rubbery spree,
Invites me over for a cup of tea.
With worms in ties, they plan their ruse,
To become the next big news!

I laugh as roots wrap 'round my shoe,
While trees perform a jig or two.
With each step, I trip on purpose,
To make the flowers laugh in surplus!

Though tethered firm to earth's embrace,
I find the humor in this space.
For every stumble has its fun,
In a world where whimsy's never done.

The Rise and Fall of Inspiration

Inspiration strikes like lightning bold,
But often leaves you feeling cold.
A spark ignites, then fizzles out,
Like a big idea chased by doubt.

I scribble notes on color-coded pads,
Yet all I get are silly fads.
Each thought is teased, then runs away,
"Oh look! A cat!"—and that's my day.

Up and down, like a yo-yo spun,
I chase the muse, just for fun!
It waves goodbye, then plays a game,
Of hide-and-seek, then calls my name.

So here I sit, with coffee in hand,
Dreaming of castles made of sand.
For in this rise, and fall, I see,
The joy of trying—just let me be.

Horizons Within Reach

The cat jumped high, oh what a sight,
Chasing dust motes, in morning light.
He missed the shelf, what a silly fall,
Landed on the dog, the king of all.

Coffee spills may dance a jig,
As I leap to dodge, oh, how big!
The floor is lava, or so I claim,
In this wild world, it's all a game.

From my desk, I spy a snack,
Can't resist a sweet little hack.
Now the shelf's a mountain peak,
In this grand quest, it's fun to seek.

With each awkward climb, laughter soars,
As socks are thrown, and humor roars.
Life's just a game, a glorious reach,
In every corner, lessons teach.

Intersections of Being

In a world of angles, and a twist or two,
I stumble over shoes, such a ridiculous view.
Every corner's a dance, every wall's a stage,
Somehow I've become the star of this age.

The clock is ticking, the cat's in a race,
Over couch, through curtains, what a frantic chase!
Laughter erupts as I lose my grip,
And the remote in hand takes an unexpected trip.

To the left, a closet, to the right, a hall,
I mix up my Socks, oh what a brawl!
Living life sideways, like a puzzle in play,
Every mishap just brightens my day.

In this jumbled abode, joy's never far,
Finding humor, where the countertops are.
Twists and turns show how fun it can seem,
At these intersections, life's a dream.

Walls that Speak

Whispers of paint, stories untold,
They watch my clumsiness, daring and bold.
A picture falls down, in a comical flurry,
I laugh with the wall, oh what a hurry!

The mirror reflects my questionable moves,
As I dance with delight, my body proves.
Against the wallpaper, I'm stuck in a groove,
Can't help but chuckle, in this silly trove.

Behind every door, is a tale of surprise,
From mischief to mayhem, I see it arise.
Empty rooms echo my giggles like charms,
While I dodge the curtains with wild flailing arms.

In this realm of corners and playful embrace,
Even the shadows join in this race.
So here's to the walls, for their humor and grace,
Making my blunders a magical place.

Entities of Elevation

Look up to the shelf, there's a cookie jar,
I jump like a frog, really going far!
Trip over the rug, and the laughter erupts,
In this grand adventure, humor is sup'd.

With ladders reaching high, challenges await,
I tiptoe like ants, it's a comical fate.
A quick little reach, oh, what's that I hear?
The jingle of change, as I chase after cheer.

Upstairs is a treasure, they say of great worth,
But my slippery socks render me mirth.
As I tumble and bounce, like a rubber ball,
I find joy in journeys, through closet and hall.

So let's raise a toast, to all things that fly,
With laughter and giggles, reaching the sky.
For every misstep, a memory bright,
In this playful realm, everything's light.

Horizons Within Reach

A clumsy cat on the windowsill,
Knocks over plants with a silly thrill.
I chase her down as she leaps with grace,
Sending my coffee across the place.

Broom in one hand, a giggle in tow,
She struts around like a star in the show.
With earthy greens scattered on the floor,
We both laugh while I mop up more!

The lamp wobbles, almost gives way,
But she's unfazed, just ready to play.
Surprises lurk in the corners, I swear,
Life's better with chaos dancing in air!

So here's to the mess, the splashes, the fun,
With every mishap, we've only begun.
Most days are wild, but we take the leap,
Finding joy in the clutter we keep!

Signals from Above

Up on the shelf, a sock has appeared,
Lost in the laundry, or did it just sneered?
An old shoe is laughing, a matchbox is bright,
While dust bunnies dance in the pale moonlight.

The ceiling fan whirs like a helicopter,
I duck from the shadows, but it's just a doctor.
He checks on the plants, gives the couch a pat,
And winks at my dog, who's already fat!

Arms up in the air, a signal so clear,
Can't find the remotes? They vanished, my dear!
The rules of the house are quite jolly, indeed,
With treasures tucked away in each little crevice, I plead.

So here is a toast, to the wonders above,
Where socks and dust bunnies fit like a glove.
When things disappear, don't shed a big tear,
Just join in the hunt and give a good cheer!

Foundations and Fragments

In the pantry, I found half a cookie,
A note from the cat: she says, 'Don't be goofy!'
With crumbs on my shirt and a grin on my face,
I ponder the wisdom of this sweet little space.

Nuts and bolts in a bowl, what a find,
Do they tell tall tales, or are they just blind?
My toolbox sings songs of unfinished dreams,
While the clock in the corner just quietly beams.

The couch springs an exit, we giggle, we fall,
With cushions like pancakes piling up tall.
A cushion fort made, we're kings for a night,
With snacks as our treasure and laughter our light.

So here's to the bits that don't really fit,
The fragments of life that bring giggles and wit.
A home full of wonder, quirk, and delight,
In each little corner, there's humor in sight!

Tall Tales in Tight Spaces

In a closet, so little, lurks a monster so grand,
A sock-eating beast, or was it my hand?
With shoes stacked high, like a tower of cheer,
It whispers sweet nothings each time I come near.

I tell it my stories of woe and delight,
Of laundry gone missing and socks taking flight.
The vacuum joins in with a roar and a sweep,
As we all gather close for a chuckle and peep.

Beneath the old stairs, secrets do creep,
My cat, on a mission, goes diving in deep.
The tales that unfold in these tight little nooks,
Would fill up a library with strange little books.

So raise up a cheer for the tall tales we spin,
In corners and cupboards, let the fun begin!
As laughter reminds us, with all of its grace,
That joy can be found in each snug little space!

Stacks of Silence

In a room piled high, not a sound to be found,
Books teeter like towers, all perfectly bound.
The cat hides beneath, in a fortress of lore,
Whiskers twitching softly, she's heard this before.

Chairs in a pyramid, stacked one on top,
Each one more wobbly, I think they'll flop.
A sneeze sends them crashing, a thunderous spree,
This room's not for silence, it's chaos by decree!

Dust bunnies quiver, they know what's in store,
As laughter erupts, we can't hold it anymore.
With each little tumble, the giggles resound,
In a world built on laughter, true joy can be found.

We gather the pieces, a jigsaw of fun,
Rebuilding our silence, better when done.
As we reach for the ceiling, let joy take its flight,
In this stack of our stories, we'll share every night.

Layers of Light

Sunbeams scatter wildly, like children at play,
Each one a giggle that brightens the day.
On curtains of laughter, they dance and they sway,
Who knew so much joy could come from a ray?

A lamp once stood guard, all grumpy and grey,
Now it's wearing shades, feeling hip in a way.
Throw pillows like clouds lounge with carefree delight,
Oh, let's fill this room with layers of light!

The ceiling's an artist with strokes bold and bright,
It paints the horizon with joy and with fright.
Each shadow's a buddy, each corner a friend,
In a house full of beams, the giggles won't end.

In corners we hide, beneath glimmers and glares,
Creating our world without worries or cares.
With laughter like lanterns, the night becomes gay,
In layers of light, we'll keep sadness at bay.

A Dance of Elevation

Up on the counter, a fruit bowl does sway,
Bananas are tap-dancing, making their play.
The apples join in with a raucous delight,
Their wobble and jiggle brings joy to the night.

The ceiling fan spins, like a DJ on high,
It's grooving with rhythm, the crowd wants to fly.
Every spin and every glide is a laughable show,
A dance of elevation, come join in the flow!

With dust motes as partners, they twirl in the sun,
Each little particle knows how to have fun.
We join in the frolic, around and around,
With giggles and twirls, we leap off the ground.

As the clock strikes an hour, we end our charade,
The fruit takes a bow, the audience swayed.
In this dance of elevation, we've all learned to fly,
In a room full of laughter, we'll never say goodbye.

Beneath the Canopy

Under a blanket, a jungle appears,
Monkeys are chattering, sharing their fears.
Cushions are mountains where explorers do roam,
In this living room jungle, we've made our home.

A rug stretches out like a great savanna,
It welcomes the laughter like a warm bandanna.
With pillows as boulders, we leap and we dive,
In our plush oasis, we're happy to thrive.

The chandelier sparkles like stars in the sky,
While the cat on the bookshelf just watches us fly.
Each roar and each giggle bounces off walls,
Beneath this wide canopy, adventure enthralls.

As the sun starts to set, we gather in cheer,
Telling wild stories to all those who hear.
In our fabric-tent forest, dreams come to play,
In a world full of joy, let's dance the night away.

Gaze Upon the Summit

A cat up high, thinks it's the king,
On a tower of books, it does cling.
Sipping on tea, quite the sight,
Balancing snacks, what a delight!

A bird below, gives a warning call,
"Don't drop those crumbs, or you'll face a fall!"
Laughter erupts as the snacks take flight,
Goldfish and crackers dancing in light.

The dog looks on, with a puzzled stare,
Wonders how snacks float in the air.
A tumble and roll, oops, down they go,
Cat's shocked expression, "I didn't know!"

So cheers to the heights, the quirky and bold,
Where stories of pets and snacks unfold.

Dimensions of Space

In my tiny room, a universe grows,
With socks on the ceiling, who really knows?
Aliens meet under the bed's dark veil,
Trading lost treasures, a daydream trail.

A chair with wheels zooms past the door,
Where's it off to? Who knows anymore!
Books whisper secrets, or so they claim,
Like a gossiping wall, it's all just a game.

A rug decides it wants to dance,
Swirling around as if in a trance.
While the clock on the wall rolls its eyes,
"Can't you all see, time surely flies!"

Socks and dust bunnies, a comical crew,
With laughs and giggles, oh what to do!

From the Lowlands to the Heights

In the valley, a potato sits proud,
Waving to carrots, forming a crowd.
The tall ones laugh, "We're way up high!"
While the low ones plot, "We'll reach the sky!"

A leaf takes a chance, a fluttering leap,
Calling the veggies to jump and creep.
"Let's build a ladder, or maybe a slide,
Who needs to be tall, when fun's the ride?"

A cabbage decides to roll down low,
Lands in a puddle, puts on a show.
With giggles and squeals, they all join in,
Together they tumble, letting fun begin!

So here's to the low and tall in life,
Where laughter blooms without any strife.

Gazing at Infinity

A fish in a bowl, with dreams to explore,
Wonders about life, beyond the shore.
"Is there a dance under the moon's soft beam?
Or perhaps a treasure in a bubble's dream?"

A snail slows down, pondering the vast,
"Whoa, what's this? Is time meant to last?"
The turtle replies, with wisdom galore,
"Who knows what's out there, behind that door!"

Clouds turn to sheep, in the sky's embrace,
Bouncing along, so they quicken the pace.
The ants on the ground, busy as can be,
"Do they know we're here? We're a sight to see!"

So let's toast to dreams, both silly and grand,
In this quirky, wondrous, expanding land.

The Journey of Untamed Edges

In a room where socks play hide and seek,
The wild carpet dances, oh so chic.
A chair does the cha-cha, with flair and pride,
While crumbs below giggle, trying to hide.

The cat on the shelf thinks he's a king,
Declaring his reign with a mighty fling.
A shoe left behind in a rogue parade,
Is trampled by dust bunnies, unafraid.

Tassels on curtains sway to the beat,
As our coffee cup winks, oh what a treat!
The walls join in, with a laugh and a cheer,
Making everyday moments feel like a frontier.

So here's to the chaos, the joy it brings,
From shoes to the ceiling, oh what fun things!
With laughter as glue, every space can gleam,
In a world of the wild, let's live out the dream.

Whispers in the Gaps

Behind the fridge, sweet secrets reside,
A rogue potato that's taken a ride.
A spider spins tales from a web so tight,
As it eavesdrops on snacks, into the night.

The dust on the shelf forms a silent crew,
Creating a ruckus, with nothing to do.
A lonely sock sighs, from a wardrobe's hold,
Yearning for adventures, whimsical and bold.

Chairs whisper gossip in creaks and moans,
While the broom dreams of glory with its paper cone.
The fridge hums a tune, under fluorescent glow,
As leftovers linger and plot their next show.

In the nooks and crannies, mischief awakes,
Amongst all the laughter, the joy it makes.
With every small gap, there's a giggle and grin,
In this house full of whispers, let the fun begin!

Whispers Above the Ground

Up on the shelves, where the teacups blend,
The sugar bowl chuckles, it's all just pretend.
A lonely old lamp with a flickering flame,
Keeps secrets of shadows that dance without shame.

The ceiling fan spins with a dizzy delight,
While the clock on the wall makes time feel too tight.
A picture hangs crooked, it laughs at the scene,
Wondering if life's just a funny routine.

The light switches laugh, with a flick and a spark,
As nighttime descends, they light up the dark.
And up high the cobwebs, they sway with such grace,
Like curtains of laughter that brighten the place.

So here are the whispers, above on display,
In a space full of giggles, let's frolic and play.
For in every small corner, let's find our delight,
And fill all the moments with humor and light.

Shadows in the Space

In the corners of shadows, where mischief may bloom,
   A pen rolls away to escape from the gloom.
  The vacuum's a monster, with teeth made of glass,
    Chasing after dust, in a whirl of sass.

  A chair takes a leap, making the others sigh,
While the rug throws a party, it's time to fly high!
   The TV remote plays tricks, it likes to hide,
As we chase it around, with laughter as our guide.

   The fridge hums a tune, of leftovers past,
Those neglected meals that we're hoping won't last.
   And under the couch, the coins have a chat,
     Making plans to escape, imagine that!

In this space full of shadows, humor takes flight,
  With giggles as echoes in the warm twilight.
  So come join the dance in this playful embrace,
Where every small shadow holds a laugh in its space.

www.ingramcontent.com/pod-product-compliance
Lightning Source LLC
Chambersburg PA
CBHW060125230426
43661CB00003B/336